The
DIVORCE
Book

A permanent record of our temporary relationship

Edited by George Leborts
and the former Mrs. Leborts

First Printing October 1984

Manufactured in the United States of America

Published by Turnbull & Willoughby Publishers, Inc.
1151 W. Webster
Chicago, IL 60614

Cover Design by Bill Dillard
Special thanks to Sandra Toback

5 4 3 2 1

Based on a concept by Geryl Kramer

To Darlene . . .
> who gave me a wonderful marriage
> and a wonderful divorce . . . what more
> could a man ask for.
> > — George Leborts
> > 1984

Table of Contents

Section One

The Seed is Sown

The First Encounter

*"You made the biggest impression
on me when you _____ "*

Section Two

Love Blooms

The Best of Times

"I loved it when you _____ "

Section Three

I Love You . . .
I Love You Not

The Initial Disillusionment

*"Why did you always
have to _____ "*

Section Four

Nettles & Thorns

Your Friends, My Friends, and the Relatives

"Your friend I hated most was _____ "

Section Five

Blight

The Worst of Times

"I couldn't believe it when you wanted me to _____ "

Section Six

Crop Failure

The Break-up

"When I realized it was over, the first thing I wanted to do was _____ "

Section Seven

Pressed Flowers

Rememberances

"If it's the last thing I do,
    I'll get you for _____ "

Section Eight

Love Blooms Again

New Relationships . . .
    Same Old Problems? (a checklist)

"Next time I'll know
    enough not to _____ "

The Seed is Sown

The First Encounter

*"You made the biggest impression
on me when you _____ "*

The First Encounter

What a difference time makes! Nothing is the way it first appears to be.

Slowly I advanced into the steamy No Holds Bar. This wasn't my kind of game but I knew it had to be played. By God, I needed a date for Saturday night, and more important, I needed a serious relationship.

Almost instantly someone caught my eye. Then, as they nonchalantly moved into my territory, the banter began.

"Hi! Do you come here often?" was their opening.

Clever, I thought, vaguely recalling having heard those words before.

As the conversation continued, and the excitement began to build, I knew this could be the one.

"555-1287. That's work. 555-9843, that's home. Here, let me write it on the back of this napkin".

There were promises that the numbers would be used soon but I felt a twinge of indecision. But it has been a while since I'd met someone so charming and so attractive. Besides, I knew mom would approve.

If this scenario, or another, surprisingly similar, sounds familiar to you, then think back.

. . . was being able to file joint tax returns really worth being in the joint where the two of you met?

. . . would your life have worked out better if, the night you'd met her, you'd gone to the ballgame with the boys instead?

. . . did you really believe him when he said an automatic screw machine operator was a charming profession for a lady? Such a liberal!

. . . were you only impressed by her fantastically fragile phony front?

. . . did you fail to notice that he couldn't find a space for your number in his little black book?

. . . did you get a little nervous, at the end of that first date, when she mentioned that her uncle was a discount diamond broker?

Well, get it off your chest . . . and dump it on theirs. Fill in the blanks with your innermost beefs. Look for the clues in those early moments that might have warned you it would all lead to this.

The first time I saw you I was attracted by your

_____

_____

My first impression was that you would be

_____

_____

Boy!! Was I

_____

After our first meeting I was sure you thought I was

_____

_____

_____

The thing I remember most about our first date is

_____

_____

_____

_____

_____

_____

Now that it's too late, I realize what I failed to notice about you at first was

_____

_____

_____

_____

_____

_____

I thought dating you would be like

_____

_____

_____

_____

_____

It was actually like (see Remembrances).

The first time I kissed you I thought

_____

_____

_____

_____

_____

I will always

_____

the day I met you.

If it wasn't for

_____

we never would have met. To that person I
would like to say

_____

_____

_____

_____

_____

Before I got to know you very well I fantasized
that you

_____

_____

_____

At the end of our first date I never thought you
would

_____

_____

_____

When we first met I had to bite my tongue
to stop from telling you

_____

_____

_____

_____

_____

You made the biggest impression on me when
you

_____

_____

_____

_____

_____

To be perfectly honest, when I first laid eyes on
you my thoughts were about

_____

_____

_____

I knew ours would be more than a casual relationship when I discovered that you could

_____

_____

_____

Unfortunately, I also quickly discovered that
you

_____

_____

_____

_____

Section Two

Love Blooms
The Best of Times

"I loved it when you _____ "

The Best of Times

No doubt, there were times like this for the two of us. And it couldn't hurt to remember them.

As the sun burst gloriously into the room, I awoke realizing this was the day of days . . . my wedding day! Alone for the last time, I luxuriated between the sheets thinking back over those thrilling months that lead up to this wonderful event.

I remembered the passion (however slight) of our first embrace. And of those exhilarating nights out on the town, whenever we didn't have to dine with the family.

Then there were those endearing little notes we sent each other along with carnations for birthdays and Valentine's Day. Never mind that everyone else was always sending roses.

Best of all was the look of envy I would read on the faces of our wedding guests. I knew they would be thinking, "these two really deserve each other!"

And what of the rapture yet to come? The honeymoon could only be perfect. Balmy nights in the Bahamas, thrilling to each other's touch. With the peace and quiet pierced, every now and then, by the sound of an office beeper or a call from mother.

Yes, no doubt there were the good times and it couldn't hurt to remember them. Salve these wounds with memories of the good old days.

. . . keep telling yourself, "I was no fool. It was right in the beginning!"

. . . who could have resisted falling in love with a man with such a magnificent income?

. . . don't let her forget that once there was high romance between the two of you.

. . . and remember that those days were filled with parties and plenty of kissing.

Set it all down on the pages that follow, then send it to the creep and listen to 'em weep.

I was happiest when

_____

_____

_____

You were most romantic when

_____

_____

_____

_____

Remember when you tried to make me

_____

_____

_____

_____

The more frequently we saw each other the more frequently we

_____

_____

_____

When

_____

heard we were getting serious, they

_____

_____

_____

After the first month of our relationship I should have

_____

_____

_____

_____

I was surprised to learn that you

_____

_____

_____

_____

_____

I was surprised to learn that you didn't

_____

_____

_____

_____

_____

I loved it when you

_____

_____

_____

_____

_____

The single thing I remember best about those "Best of Times" is

_____

_____

_____

_____

_____

_____

My fondest memory of being madly in lust with you is

_____

_____

_____

_____

_____

_____

Everyone was jealous that we were able to

_____

_____

_____

_____

_____

I would get the tingles every time you

_____

_____

_____

Even when we were madly in love, the first sign of trouble was

_____

_____

_____

_____

_____

_____

_____

When I think of our wedding vows now, I think

_____

_____

_____

_____

I had second thoughts on our honeymoon when
you

_____

_____

_____

_____

_____

Sometimes I didn't think we'd make it through
the first year when you wouldn't stop

_____

_____

_____

_____

The thing you did that turned me on the most was

_____

_____

_____

_____

_____

_____

_____

I really loved how you could

_____

at the same time you were

_____

Oh!! How you could

_____

_____

_____

_____

If I was planning our wedding ceremony now,
I'd

_____

_____

_____

_____

_____

I couldn't believe you let

_____

be in the wedding

When I heard the words, "for better or for
worse", I thought

_____

_____

_____

_____

_____

The best thing that happened on our wedding night was

_____

_____

_____

_____

_____

_____

_____

The worst thing that happened on our wedding night was

_____

_____

_____

_____

_____

_____

_____

Our honeymoon reminded me of

_____

_____

_____

The wedding gift I couldn't believe you liked
was

_____

As a married couple, I think we reminded most
people of

_____

The best thing about sex with you was your
ability to

_____

_____

The sweetest thing you ever said was

_____

My fondest memory of our wedding ceremony is

_____

_____

_____

_____

_____

_____

____ _____

My fondest memory of our wedding night is

_____

_____

_____

_____

_____

_____

_____

Section Three

I Love You . . .
I Love You Not

The Initial
Disillusionment

"Why did you always
have to _____ "

The Initial Disillusionment

Why didn't we see the handwriting on the wall when those little things began to bother us in a big way?

We'd heard it said of us so many times, "What a dashing couple." But before I knew it, we were both dashing off to something (or somebody) more interesting.

I found myself thinking back to the early days. To those romantic evenings in that cozy little apartment when our sex life wasn't yet legal (but more fun) and our quiet dinners for two still had all the nice touches.

The only touches now seem to be taken for granted and the little niceties have disappeared.

Too many late night poker parties with the boys? Too many late night tupperware parties with the girls? We both should have seen the handwriting on the wall.

. . . can you remember when the fire began to die? And when we started flinging buckets of water on it?

. . . do thoughts of how the relationship began to sour leave a sour taste in your mouth?

. . . do you recall discovering that his desire for you was totally undesirable?

. . . could you really believe the girl you married wasn't anything quite like the girl you thought you were marrying?

Well, don't just think back and enlighten yourself alone. Furiously fill in the section that's next, then have it copied and sent to your ex.

Couldn't you see the handwriting on the wall when

_____

_____

Didn't you get the message when

_____

told you that

_____

_____

The chemistry and passion began to go out of
our lives when

_____

_____

You embarrassed me most when you

_____

_____

I never understood how you could have

_____

_____

_____

I got the first inkling something was wrong when

_____

_____

_____

_____

_____

Why did you always have to

_____

_____

_____

We probably could have saved our relationship if we would have

_____

_____

_____

_____

_____

_____

I wish we would have because

_____

_____

I'm glad we didn't because

_____

_____

_____

I hate to admit it but I was really

_____

_____

when I told you I was

_____

_____

Do you think I really believed you when you told me

_____

_____

I began to have second thoughts when I
discovered that you couldn't

_____

as well as you thought you could.

Even when I started

_____

more than usual, you didn't get the message.

I always dreamed that I would marry someone
who would

_____

_____

but I started to realize that you

_____

_____

_____

_____

I couldn't believe it when you wanted me to

_____

_____

_____

I noticed our relationship starting to cool when
you started to

_____

_____

_____

_____

_____

If my father found out that you wanted me to

_____

he would have

_____

_____

_____

I always had a sneaking suspicion you were
really

_____

_____

when you said you were

_____

_____

I couldn't believe it when I discovered you liked
to

_____

_____

_____

I sure was sure surprised to learn that you
didn't like to

_____

_____

_____

Nettles & Thorns

Your Friends, My Friends and the Relatives

"Your friend I hated
    most was _____ "

Your Friends, My Friends . . . and the Relatives

Why didn't everyone leave us alone? . . . those well meaning inlaws and busybody friends . . .

It was a joyous time of the year, when the snow covered everything with a fine glittering film. All the creatures . . . best of all, the in-laws . . . had flown to Florida and it was time to give thanks for making it through another year with just a minimum of major familial battles.

After gorging ourselves on burnt bird and underdone mincemeat, we spent the evening planning our usual year-end bash, trying desperately not to bash each other.

We always liked to keep these parties intimate with no more than 300 of our dearest friends. That is, of course, in addition to the relatives. When it came to parties we always listened to our mothers, "The more invited, the more delighted!" "Wasn't mother charming?", I winced.

Of course all of the "girls" and the "boys" would be invited. The girls who all got their hair done, nails done, feet done, eyes tucked and skin nipped together. And there were the boys. The golf gang. They were par for the course.

And one mustn't leave out Rhoda and Wade. Why, they were our first friends as a couple! With a grimace, I wondered, "Who would get them in the settlement?"

. . . were your parties planned with such panache?

. . . did your parents plan to puncture your mate's holiday hilarity?

. . . did your family and friends add meaning to your major Fall feuds?

. . . was your mother-in-law really that bad, that you had to lay into her and make your ex so mad?

. . . would it have been smarter not to let your best friend spend so much time around the house? Maybe you wouldn't have lost your spouse.

Be sure to let your estranged spouse know! Writing it down will give you a reason, to send your former partner something next holiday season.

The family gathering you screwed up the most was

_____

_____

_____

_____

_____

_____

I couldn't believe it when your parents

_____

_____

_____

_____

_____

It's now plain to see that your relatives are direct descendants of

_____

_____

All of the jokes about mother-in-laws are

_____

_____

I never knew what interference was until

_____

_____

_____

_____

When our friends would get together

_____

would always screw things up

_____

Every time your mother would

_____

I wanted to

_____

Your worst trait I can blame on your father is

_____

_____

_____

_____

_____

_____

The first time you called your mother was

_____

_____

_____

_____

Of all your friends, I disliked

_____

the most because

_____

_____

_____

Would you believe that

_____

made a pass at me!??!

And I

_____

_____

_____

_____

_____

Your worst trait that I can blame on your mother is

_____

_____

_____

_____

_____

When I told

_____

we were getting serious, they said

_____

_____

_____

_____

warned me in advance that I should be concerned about your tendency to

_____

_____

_____

_____

The worst thing your parents did for our relationship was

_____

_____

_____

I think the major problem with the way you choose your friends is

_____

_____

_____

_____

_____

_____

I know that

_____

never liked me because

_____

_____

_____

was the first to guess that we weren't going to make it.

The best thing your parents did for our relationship was

_____

_____

_____

_____

_____

Compared to

_____

your parents were

_____

_____

_____

_____

When it comes to the marriage of their children, I think all parents should

_____

_____

_____

_____

_____

_____

All of my friends thought you were

_____

_____

I didn't have the heart to tell them you were really

_____

_____

_____

_____

Section Five

Blight
The Worst of Times

*"I couldn't believe it when
you wanted me to _____ "*

The Worst of Times

Everyone kept saying, "things could be worse", but I couldn't imagine how they could have been.

The day finally arrived when I realized our love was a lie. Although that miserably dismal day fit my mood like a boxing glove, the excitement level of the moment was high. So what if there was no fun left in the relationship . . . there could still be some fun left in the fighting!

Everything seemed to fall apart. We lost the trust we once had; you lost your sex drive and your nice body as well. I lost interest and may have strayed a bit (but we won't go into that now).

The fights. Oh what fights! Big ones, little ones, serious ones, silly ones. OK. I'll admit you didn't start them all . . . but you certainly caused them all.

Like ours, did your clashes classify as world title tussles?

. . . did the wedding bells signal the start of round one?

. . . were the inconsiderations of prize-winning proportions?

. . . was she as fast with her lashing tongue as Ali was fast on his feet?

. . . or did he merely cheat because the low blow was his style of being indiscreet?

If you can answer yes to any of the questions above, you are eligible to enter your gripes in the spaces provided. Just be sure not to pull any punches. Give it to 'em good! At the sound of the bell, return for your pencils and come out writing!

Every time a fight started I could always count on you to

_____

_____

_____

_____

Our biggest fight was

_____

_____

_____

_____

Our longest fight was

_____

_____

_____

_____

_____

I knew it was all over when

_____

_____

_____

_____

_____

I'll never forget the scene you made when

_____

_____

_____

_____

_____

I always knew a fight was coming when you

_____

_____

_____

_____

I got tired of always having you compare me to

_____

_____

You were most inconsiderate when you

_____

_____

_____

_____

The part of your body that made me laugh most
was

_____

because

_____

_____

_____

_____

Our stupidest fight was

_____

_____

_____

_____

_____

The first time my eyes went astray was

_____

_____

_____

_____

The first time I cheated on you was

_____

_____

_____

_____

The thing you did that turned me off the most was

_____

_____

_____

_____

_____

When I used to come home late and tell you I was at

_____

I was really at

_____

It seemed you were only horney when

_____

_____

_____

You embarrassed me most when you

_____

_____

_____

_____

You should be eternally indebted to me for putting up with your

_____

_____

_____

_____

Your biggest indiscretion was

_____

_____

_____

_____

And all you ever offered was

_____

If you knew how

_____

you looked when you

_____

you'd probably

_____

Every time you

_____

I couldn't help but

_____

because you seemed so

_____

It seemed you were never horney when

_____

_____

_____

I wish you would have spent more time

_____ing,

instead of

_____ing.

As everyone knows, your worst personal habit is

_____

_____

When we fought you never learned that I needed someone who

_____

_____

You always seemed so righteous when you told me I should

_____

and all the time you were.

You thought you were real cute when you would

_____

but I thought you

_____

_____

The longer we stayed together the more my friends thought I was a

_____

In the morning I always thought you would look like

_____

but I soon discovered you looked like

_____

instead.

We would still be together today if you would have

_____

_____

We would still be together today if I would have

_____

_____

_____

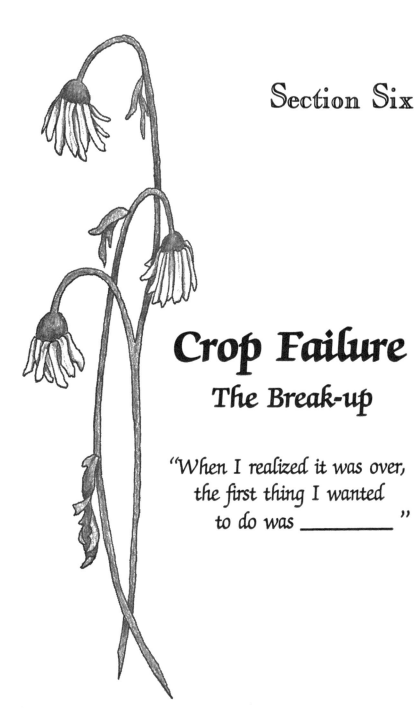

Crop Failure
The Break-up

*"When I realized it was over,
the first thing I wanted
to do was _____ "*

The Break-up

I never believed it would end like this. But guess what? . . . it did!

I returned to the lonely lair where I'd been living since being banished from our home. I was beginning to doubt the wisdom of my former follies. After all, we were good parents. And what would become of the children?

As my thoughts intensified, I absent mindedly leafed through my pile of mail. "What's this? Another huge bill from Visa? And who are Feinstein, Scheinberg and Kissoff?" Oh well, I guess someone had to take the first step. Now it was actually happening. We had discussed who was going to take care of the laundry but I didn't expect to be taken to the cleaners!

Generally speaking, I had been a good spouse and this is the treatment I get? The barracudas had been hired and they suggested I have my own shark call them. I have a feeling I know who is going to get the smaller share.

. . . do you remember a summons of this sort? Or do you remember sending one?

. . . to avoid future contact, have you changed the locks and unlisted the phone? And do you feel the judge was a stupid old crone?

. . . were you worried that if he took the kids, they'd take after him?

. . . were you really unpleasantly surprised when you discovered she wasn't willing to compromise?

. . . when he pleaded poverty in court, did you subtly mention he was driving a newly polished Porsche?

Well, don't let such thoughts make you so mad, just write them all down on this handy little pad.

Even though I knew it was coming, the most shocking thing about the actual break-up was

_____

_____

_____

_____

My first night alone after our break up is best described as

_____

_____

_____

_____

_____

For appearances, I tried to look like I was

_____

but deep down inside I felt like

_____

When I told

_____

that we were breaking up they said

_____

_____

When I finally realized that it was all over, the first thing I wanted to do was

_____

_____

_____

_____

It is going to take me

_____

_____

to get over our relationship.

When I left the courtroom that day I felt like

_____

_____

_____

_____

But after a few drinks I felt like

_____

_____

_____

_____

In my opinion, our settlement is

_____

_____

_____

_____

_____

_____

I never took you seriously when you talked about breaking up until you

_____

_____

_____

_____

After hearing so much about messy divorces, I couldn't believe ours was

_____

_____

_____

_____

Negotiating with you and your lawyer was like

_____

_____

_____

_____

_____

I'll never forgive you for taking the

_____

when you left.

You were such a

_____

about the whole   thing.

If I ever run into you again don't be surprised if I

_____

_____

_____

_____

_____

Could you believe it when the judge said

_____

_____

_____

_____

I couldn't believe you fought so hard for the

_____

in the settlement because I really didn't give
a damn about it.

Your traits I hope the children don't inherit are

_____

_____

_____

_____

_____

_____

_____

Section Seven

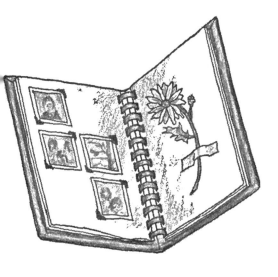

Pressed Flowers

Remembrances

*"If it's the last thing I do,
I'll get you for* _____

Remembrances

Whenever I think of the two of us now, I can still remember the sweet along with the bitter.

Could I ever forget the way things once had been? Had I been kind or some kind of nut? I couldn't be sure at the moment.

Every time I encounter someone who bears even the slightest physical resemblance to my ex, I can't help but remember . . . both the good times and the bad. And when I am alone at night (although it isn't very often) I still reminisce about those days gone by, sometimes not believing I made it through them.

The thought that plagued me most was that all our friends had thought us such a perfect couple. Did they look at both of us in the same way? God! I'd have to change my entire personality.

"STOP!!" I told myself. The time had come to forget the jerk and begin planning for the future.

. . . can't you stop thinking about your last legal lover?

. . . were you most misunderstood when you were trying hardest to be good?

. . . will it be your eternal fate, never to forget your first mate?

. . . when you're alone and feeling really bad, do you have to force yourself to block out thoughts of those one or two good days the two of you had?

Even if you pray each day for a minor case of amnesia, don't fall victim yet. Maybe one more round of remembrances, for posterity, will finally get it out of your system.

The things about our marriage I won't miss at all are

_____

_____

_____

_____

_____

_____

After all the time we spent together, what you STILL misunderstand about me most is

_____

_____

_____

On the other hand, what I think I misunderstood most about you was

_____

_____

_____

_____

Remember the time we

_____

all day long?

If I had just one memory to choose, the fondest
memory of our marriage would be

_____

_____

_____

_____

_____

Remember all the times I wanted to

_____

_____

and you wanted to

_____

_____

You made me most proud when you

_____

_____

_____

_____

You were most understanding when

_____

_____

_____

_____

_____

You were least understanding when

_____

_____

_____

_____

_____

If and when I ever fantasize about you it's about

_____

_____

_____

_____

Even today, every time I see a

_____

I   think of you.

You were the biggest baby when

_____

_____

_____

About that time I got so mad at you that I hit you. I would like to

_____

_____

I will always cherish the

_____

you gave me.

In my opinion, your most underestimated trait
is

_____

_____

_____

_____

_____

In my opinion, your most overestimated trait is

_____

_____

_____

_____

_____

Your best physical attribute is

_____

_____

_____

_____

Your worst physical attribute is

_____

_____

_____

_____

Your optimum weight is

_____

If you still own that

_____

burn it!!

If you only would have tried a little harder you would have been much better at

_____

_____

_____

_____

If it's the last thing I do I'll get you for

_____

_____

_____

_____

The worst thing anyone ever said about you was

_____

_____

_____

_____

The best thing about your love making technique is

_____

_____

_____

_____

_____

_____

The worst thing about your lovemaking technique is

_____

_____

_____

_____

_____

_____

I almost gagged when you said that

_____

_____

_____

was part of a serious relationship.

You were so helpless when it came to

_____

_____

_____

_____

I would have liked it better if you could have

_____

_____

just half as good as you could

_____

_____

The best thing anyone ever said about you was

_____

_____

_____

_____

_____

The truest thing anyone ever said about you was

_____

_____

_____

_____

I still tingle when I remember how you used to

_____

_____

_____

_____

_____

The one thing about you that I find most difficult to forget is

_____

_____

_____

If you would have been more

_____

_____

_____

I wouldn't have always been so

_____

Seriously, all joking aside, I wish you had been able to

_____

_____

Seriously, all joking aside, I wish I would have been able to

_____

_____

Love Blooms Again

New Relationships . . . Same Old Problems? (a checklist)

"Next time I'll know
enough not to _____ "

New Relationships . . . Same Old Problems?

I can say one thing with great certainty: "The mistakes I made the first time around will be much different from the mistakes I make next time!"

It had been a smashing evening. I was on the prowl again. The music. The lights. The laughter. The people were completely different from you-know-who.

But were they?!

I'd been so sure that first time around. This time I'd be smarter. I wouldn't wear my heart on my sleeve. This time I won't even bother with sleeves; maybe something a bit more chic.

I'd learn to say what I really meant and set the rules in the beginning. I won't give in to my desires until the trap is really set. After one disastrous relationship, I'm sure I know exactly what I'm looking for.

. . . were you a prisoner of your own passions. Or of your first spouse's lack of them?

. . . can you now tell the difference between marriage material and material wealth?

. . . will the mistakes you made the first time around help you avoid hooking up with an even bigger clown?

. . . can you confidently say, that in the future you'd do it a different way?

. . . did your wife make the world safe for all the women who ever said they weren't ready for a serious relationship with you?

. . . when you said, I wish we could afford a new desk, did he make you go to work at one?

. . . Then take a moment now to catalog the errors. Don't say it will never happen again. It's out there just waiting to happen. Consider the path you took to your former demise, so next time around you'll be a bit more wise.

Your best attribute your new lover will find
most enjoyable is

_____

_____

_____

_____

_____

If your new dates think you're as

_____

_____

as you think you are, they are

_____

_____

If you are still

_____

_____

your new relationships don't stand a chance.

One thing I used to do a lot with you that I'm going to be doing more of with

_____

is

_____

_____

_____

_____

One thing I used to do a lot with you that I'm not going to do with

_____

is

_____

_____

_____

_____

My guess is your new lovers will mistakenly think you are

_____

_____

until they get to know you as well as I do.

If I had just 30 seconds to talk to your new financee before your next wedding, I'd say

_____

_____

_____

_____

_____

_____

Next time I'll know enough not to

_____

_____

_____

Remember how I always said my next lover wouldn't

_____

_____

Well, they don't.

I think the biggest mistake you will make when you start to date again is

_____

_____

_____

_____

_____

_____

I think we started

_____

_____

too early in our relationship. Next time around I think I'll wait a little longer.

If you ever run into me and my date, the biggest difference you will notice in me is

_____

_____

_____

_____

They say that love is lovlier the second time around. I think it's

_____

_____

_____

The fault you should work on most before you think about getting married again is

_____

_____

_____

_____

_____

Starting a new relationship is like

_____

_____

_____

_____

_____

The biggest difference between you and the people I'm dating now is

_____

_____

_____

_____

_____

My new lovers are thankful to you because all of your bitching and complaining has caused me to stop

_____

_____

You never believed me when I told you that you were

_____

_____

_____

but now that you are on your own you'll realize that

_____

_____

_____

_____

I should learn to place more emphasis on people who

_____

_____

Next time I fall madly in love I'll make sure it's with someone who can

_____

as well as you can

The next time I fall in love, I'll make sure it's with someone who doesn't

_____

_____

like you do

If I'm smart, next time I won't say

_____

_____

_____

I'll just think it.

If I'm smart, next time I won't let my friends
and relatives

_____

_____

_____

If I'm smart, next time I'll learn to say

_____

_____

even though I really mean

_____

_____

Checklist

If I'm smart, next time I won't be so

_____

_____

If I'm smart, next time I'll be more

_____

_____

If I'm smart, next time I won't be so impressed by

_____

_____

_____

If I'm smart, next time I won't put up with

_____

_____

_____

If I'm smart, next time I won't

_____

_____

until first I

_____

_____

If I'm smart, even if I run into someone I care for as much as I cared for you, I'll know enough not to

_____

_____

_____

If I'm smart, I'll realize that next time I'll probably make the same mistakes all over again.